NUMBER TWO
Essays on the American West
sponsored by the
Elma Dill Russell Spencer Foundation

The Trader on the American Frontier

The Trader
ON THE
American Frontier
Myth's Victim

BY

Howard R. Lamar

Drawings by Kristin Emig Parsons

TEXAS A&M UNIVERSITY PRESS

College Station and London

Library of Congress Cataloging in Publication Data

Lamar, Howard Roberts.
    The trader on the American frontier.

    (Essays on the American West; no. 2)
    1. The West—Commerce—History. 2. Frontier and
pioneer life—The West. I. Title II. Series.
HF3159.L35   381′.0978   76-51650
ISBN 0-89096-033-X

Manufactured in the United States of America
FIRST EDITION

To Ralph Henry Gabriel

These people [the Mandans] are in the habit of seeing no white men in their country but Traders, and know of no other; deeming us all alike, and receiving us all under the presumption that we come to trade or barter; applying to us all, indiscriminately, the epithet of "liars" or Traders.

The reader will therefore see, that we mutually suffer in each other's estimation from the unfortunate ignorance, which distance has chained us in; and (as I can voice, and the Indian also, who has visited the civilized world) that the historian who would record justly and correctly the character and customs of a people, must go and live among them.

George Catlin
"Letter No. 11" in *Letters and Notes on the Manners, Customs, and Conditions of North American Indians*

The Trader on the American Frontier

The Trader

ON THE

American Frontier
Myth's Victim

IN April, 1849, a rambunctious young Texas bachelor named Benjamin Butler Harris set out for the California gold mines with a group of friends. Harris chose to take the Southern Trail across Texas, New Mexico, and Arizona to southern California as his route to the new El Dorado. Soon after he started, Harris and his party met fifteen Comanche Indians and five or six Mexican boy herders driving about five hundred Mexican horses and mules to Torrey's trading station on the Brazos.[1] Torrey's Post, some eight miles below Waco, was the most important trading house in the history of the Brazos frontier. Though the firm was backed by New England capital, General Sam Houston was a shareholder.[2]

[1] Benjamin Butler Harris, *The Gila Trail: The Texas Argonauts and the California Gold Rush*, ed. and ann. Richard H. Dillon (Norman: University of Oklahoma Press, 1960), pp. 35–37.

[2] Rupert N. Richardson, *The Comanche Barrier to South Plains Settlement* (Glendale, Calif.: Arthur H. Clark Company, 1933), p. 128 n, describes the trading house as six miles southeast of present-day Waco. Richard H. Dillon places the post "on the east bank of the Brazos eight miles below Waco. . . ." The post was one of several established by three brothers, John F., David K., and Thomas S. Torrey (Harris, *The Gila Trail*, p. 35 n). Torrey's Trading House is described in Ferdinand Roemer, *Texas* (English edition, San Antonio: Standard Printing Company, 1935), pp. 191–196.

The Indians came into Harris' camp, where "at night," wrote Harris, "we had an interchange of amusements. The Indians entertained us with their songs, accompanied with shot shaken in gourds, with war whoops and jumping (which they think is dancing), after which we, in turn, with violin music danced cotillions upon the green prairie, each Indian dancer being the gentleman and each white representing the lady. I, in my cowskin boots, was introduced to a chief as "Miss Harris" and became his partner in the "light fantastic toe" performance. The chief had by way of ornament a skunk's tail fastened to his scalp lock, whose performance was far "louder" than that diffused by any ballroom dude or coquette. What a travesty! What a mocking of calisthenic exercises followed!" The bucks, Harris explained, did not understand the calls and thus "had to be slung and twisted about by their 'lady' partners, jerked this way and that through the figures until at last we gave up in fatigued merriment and retired for the night."[3]

Aside from the enormous Freudian implications of a Texan playing a "lady" to an Indian chief, what is the significance of Harris' meeting with the Comanches? It is that when the festivities were over, some sobering facts about the nature of frontier trade came to light. The Mexican boy herders told Harris and his friends that their entire town had been wiped out by the Comanches and that the horses and mules they had with them were stolen property. It soon became clear that the boys themselves were captives of the Indians. The gold-

[3] Harris, *The Gila Trail*, pp. 35–36. For a convenient account of the Comanches, see Ernest Wallace and E. Adamson Hoebel, *The Comanches, Lords of the Plains* (Norman: University of Oklahoma Press, 1952).

seekers wanted to ambush the Indians and kill them in revenge, but one of their leaders, Captain Samuel M. Parry, and David K. Torrey, who was present, said that such an act could start an Indian war. Instead Torrey bought the boys from the Comanches, and one assumes he bought the animals as well, for Harris noted that Torrey regularly bought goods the Indians had stolen from the Mexican settlements.[4]

The episode epitomized the difference in attitudes between the frontier trader and the nontrading American settler. Harris himself reflected the views of Colonel Harvey Mitchell, a Brazos pioneer, who told them at the

[4] Harris reported that the Torreys had three posts: one "on the Brazos, one at Presidio, and one on the upper Red River." Each of these traded in stolen goods from Mexico (*The Gila Trail*, p. 37). The farflung mercantile activities of the Torreys are mentioned in John K. Strecker, "Chronicles of George Barnard, The Indian Trader of the Tehuacana and Other Bits of Texas History," *The Baylor Bulletin* 31 (September, 1928), 1–58. Barnard and the Torreys had been childhood schoolmates in Hartford, Connecticut, and were business partners in various enterprises in Texas. For more information on Barnard, see Roger N. Conger, *Highlights of Waco History* (Waco: Texian Press, 1945), pp. 75–81.

outset of their journey "to shoot at every Indian we saw and save them the life of misery in subsisting on snakes, skunks and other disgusting objects."[5] Colonel Mitchell was at least right about skunks. Harris saw the traders in an equally unfavorable light. He felt that Torrey's trading posts were "a curse to Mexico—then at peace with us—and a stimulus to robbery and murder of her people. The Torreys and their trade were, if not the prime factor, the spurs to all this ferocious deviltry."[6]

The Torreys, on the other hand, undoubtedly saw the Comanches as customers and probably as human beings. But our mythic image of such traders has been shaped by American cultural norms and by western movies, which portray them as despicable characters cavorting with Indians and supplying them with guns. In film portrayals the trader usually has a lecherous eye for both the white and the Indian heroine. Yet the Torreys were Connecticut Yankees from a prominent Hartford family and during the 1840's assisted Houston in reversing Mirabeau B. Lamar's disastrous Indian policy of hostility toward the Comanches.[7]

While Harris and the rest of us tend to see the Torreys from a settler's point of view, there was, in fact, a trader's point of view, indeed, a trader's world in North America that lasted from 1600 to 1850. That world has been ignored in our histories of the frontier, although we have full accounts of various frontier enterprises such as the fur trade and the Santa Fe trade. But these

5 Harris, *The Gila Trail*, p. 31 n. Mitchell later was influential in bringing the Agricultural and Mechanical College of Texas (now Texas A&M University) to Brazos County. Dillon's identification of Harris's "Colonel Harvey" as Mitchell is tentative.

6 *Ibid.*, p. 37.

7 Richardson, *The Comanche Barrier*, pp. 117–137.

enterprises are seen as romantic, episodic, temporary, a mere preface to settlement. Both the fur trade and the Santa Fe trade have been seen as a time of adventure, color, and violence before reality sets in. Still, in the history of the trans-Mississippi West the trader and trade relations were the key to Indian-white relations from 1600 to 1850, a period longer than that of our nation's existence.

In re-examining the main determinants of frontier history, I would like to argue that we have neglected a dual tradition of trade and mercantile capitalism by overstressing the mythic figures of explorers, pioneers, and settlers. On the frontier trade meant many things. Our friend Harris, for example, was understandably shocked at the sale of Mexican children, yet he was actually witnessing the variation of a prehistoric trade which had gone on in the Southwest for centuries. When Coronado came to New Mexico in 1540–1541, he found slaves from the Caddoan villages of Kansas living in the Pueblo towns of New Mexico.[8] Soon after Santa Fe was settled by the Spanish, the governors of that province began trafficking in Indian slaves who were sent to work in the mines of Chihuahua. Cabeza de Vaca, who had himself been enslaved by Texas Indians, was delighted when he encountered Indians fleeing from Spanish slave-hunting parties for, said he, "we gave many

<hr />

[8] George P. Hammond and Agapito Rey, eds., *Narratives of the Coronado Expedition*, Coronado Historical Series, vol. II (Albuquerque: University of New Mexico Press, 1940), 188, 219, 234–237.

thanks to God our Lord. Having almost despaired of finding Christians again, we could hardly restrain our excitement."[9]

From the seventeenth century to the 1860's captured Indian slaves did the work in many New Mexican households. The Spanish themselves had plugged into a general trade system that already existed between the Pueblo Indians and the Plains tribes. Central to that exchange were bison products which were bartered for cotton blankets and maize, but slaves were also an item of intertribal trade. One of the centers of the trade was Pecos, but others were to be found at Taos, Picurís, and San Juan as well. By 1630 the governor was sending expeditions into the Texas Panhandle to trade for hides. Since much of the trade was with the eastern Lipan Apaches, the Spanish tried to placate them and gave them a most-favored-nation status. There were periodic violent fights between Spaniard and Indian, but both sides continued to be governed by the trading motive, so much so that it appears the Spanish even let certain Apaches have horses in order to foster the hide trade.[10]

The Apache and Navaho groups living west of the Rio Grande were not treated well, in part because they had nothing to trade. Instead, the Navahos were raided

[9] Cabeza de Vaca, *Adventures in the Unknown Interior of America* (New York: Macmillan, 1972), trans. and ann. Cyclone Covey, pp. 122–125.

[10] Charles W. Hackett, ed., *Historical Documents Relating to New Mexico, Nueva Viscaya, and Approaches Thereto, to 1773 . . . ,* 3 vols. (Washington, D.C.: The Carnegie Institution of Washington, 1923), III, 140, 156, 161–162. For a reinterpretation of the traffic in slaves I am indebted to Jane E. Scott, "New Aspects of the Indian Slave Trade: Indian Contributions to Commerce in New Mexico, 1540–1775" (paper presented December, 1975, Yale University).

as a source of slaves. Trade with the eastern Apache continued after the Pueblo Revolt of 1680 until they were largely replaced by a rising trade between Spanish *comancheros* and the Comanches.[11] By concentrating on the history of black slavery in the United States, historians have ignored the existence in the Southwest of an older, more classic form of slavery that had existed in Africa, Asia, Greece, and Rome, in which captives were incoporated into households and often became a part of the tribe or nation that had captured them.

Meanwhile the Spanish horse had spread up from New Mexico both onto the Great Plains and into the Great Basin of Utah. One of the tribes on the northeastern edge of the Great Basin who got horses were the ancestors of the Comanches, who then moved from the Rocky Mountains to eastern Colorado.[12] In this same period Pawnee Indians on the eastern side of the central plains secured guns from French traders and spread them westward. These developments eventually caused a new shift in population, for the Comanches and Utes drove

11 The Spanish alliance with the Comanches began in the 1780's and continued through the period of Mexican rule in the Southwest (see Charles L. Kenner, *A History of New Mexican–Plains Indian Relations* [Norman: University of Oklahoma Press, 1969], ch. 4, "The Comanchero Trade, 1786–1860"). The extraordinary range of trade in goods, animals, and captives is traced in Elizabeth Ann Harper, "The Taovayas Indians in Frontier Trade and Diplomacy, 1769–1779," *Southwestern Historical Quarterly* 57 (October, 1953), 181–201; and J. Evetts Haley, "The Comanchero Trade," *ibid.* 38 (January, 1935), 157–176. See also Carl Coke Rister, *Border Captives: The Traffic in Prisoners by Southern Plains Indians, 1835–1857* (Norman: University of Oklahoma Press, 1940), and the same author's *Comanche Bondage* (Glendale, Calif.: Arthur H. Clark Company, 1955).

12 Francis Haines, *The Plains Indians, Their Origins, Migrations and Cultural Development* (New York: Thomas Y. Crowell Company, 1976), details the movements of all the Plains tribes.

the eastern Apache south and the Comanches began trading with New Mexicans at Taos, where they provided Kiowa, Jumano, Pawnee, and Apache slaves to the Spanish and to the Pueblos. A witness in Taos described the trading:

> Here the governor, alcaldes and lieutenants gather together as many horses as they can; here is collected all the ironwork possible, such as axes, hoes, wedges, picks, bridles, machetes, belduques and knives . . . for trade and barter with these barbarians in exchange for deer and buffalo hides, and for Indian slaves, men and women, small and large, a great multitude of both sexes.[13]

When the new Republic of Mexico let American traders come to Santa Fe and Taos after 1821, a Euro-Indian trading system some two hundred years old was already in operation.[14] Indians were used to traders when Bent's Fort was built on the Arkansas in 1833 and when Torrey's Post in Texas was founded in 1843. As many as 20,000 Indians might gather first at Bent's to trade and then a portion of them might move on to Tor-

---

[13] Hackett, *Historical Documents*, III, 442, 453, 494.

[14] See Jack D. Forbes, *Apache, Navaho and Spaniard* (Norman: University of Oklahoma Press, 1960). "They [a family of Utes] took us for traders and they brought chamois skins and other things for exchange; among these they brought preserves made of small black apples . . . which were very similar to grapes and very tasty. We convinced the Indians, though they did not believe us altogether, that we were not traders" (Fr. Silvestre Velez de Escalante, August 24, 1776, quoted in Frank McNitt, *The Indian Traders* [Norman: University of Oklahoma Press, 1972], p. xv).

rey's.[15] Some of the horses the Indians had might be sent by relay-barter system up to the Sioux tribes in the Dakotas. These posts and those which sprang up on the Missouri were not only the meeting ground for red and white; they were, as John Ewers tells us, an Indian recreation center, a bank, credit union, pawn shop, and even a health and welfare outpost all rolled into one organization.[16] One can almost hear a condescending Indian telling a friend: "We have this little log post down by the riverfront, where you can get excellent drinks. The proprietor, a paleface, charges too much—you know how grasping they are—but man, it's where the action is."

This imaginary scene, full of linguistic anachronisms, is deliberate because one of the first victims of the accounts of the trader's frontier is that the Indian was himself a victim with no ability to trade or get what he wanted. The fact is that the Plains tribes traded with whites from 1700 to 1850 without a notable deterioration of their culture and strength except by disease after the smallpox epidemics of 1837. During this time at least seven generations traded without losing their culture or tribal identity. On the white side traders took pains to find out what the Indians liked and did not like. Fort Union traders on the upper Missouri were upset that the white beads they had ordered were all blue.

15 Ferdinand Roemer, *Texas*, p. 193, describes a Comanche trade in mules which appear to have come from the New Mexico region. David Lavender, *Bent's Fort* (Garden City, N.Y.: Doubleday & Company, 1954), is a fine account of this important trading center.

16 John C. Ewers, "The Influence of the Fur Trade upon the Indians of the Northern Plains," in Malvina Bolus, ed., *People and Pelts* (Winnipeg: Peguis, 1972), pp. 6–7.

They reported to their suppliers that the Indians wanted a large trigger guard on the guns so they could be shot by a mittened finger. We also learn that Indians played trade rivals against one another, and that some traders used Indian policemen—a kind of native security or detective agency to keep order at the posts.[17]

Even before the white trading posts came to the Missouri Valley, the Mandan and Hidatsa villages in the vicinity of present-day Bismarck, North Dakota, were the Pecoses and Taoses of the north. There the Mandans sold corn to the Assiniboine Indians in return for meat and hides. Indians to their east sold the Mandans French or British guns at 100 percent markup, which they resold to those west and south of them at another 100 percent markup. Meanwhile, the Crow, having gotten horses from Great Basin tribes, sold Mandan horses at a fantastic markup. In turn the Mandan and other middleman tribes sold the horses at an equally fantastic markup to the Assiniboine or Cree.[18] The concept of the Indian middleman, so well developed in studies of the Iroquois and the fur trade, has not been fully explored as a factor in trade relations with western tribes.[19]

Among other things, trade in horses meant that an elaborate north-south trade network existed in the Great Basin which supplied Shoshonean Indians on its northern edge with so many horses they became sophisticated deal-

17 *Ibid.*, pp. 10, 12, 17.
18 *Ibid.*, pp. 2–4.
19 See George T. Hunt, *The Wars of the Iroquois* (Madison: University of Wisconsin Press, 1940), and Allen W. Trelease, *Indian Affairs in Colonial New York* (Ithaca, N.Y.: Cornell University Press, 1960), for convenient summaries of the Iroquois fur trade.

ers in trading with tribes to the north and east of them.[20] Some of these groups provided horses that sped Lewis and Clark on their historic journey to the Pacific coast in 1805.

By the nineteenth century a truly great horsetrader had emerged in the Great Basin: the Ute Chief Walkara, whom the whites called "Walker." This handsome, hawk-nosed leader, who mixed European finery and Indian costume and had so many bells on his horses that his entourage sounded like a rhythm band, organized a band of mounted raiders and fighters from several tribes, some of them traditional enemies, to raid California ranches for horses. These were sold to mountain men and trappers at the Green River rendezvous. In one famous raid Walkara was joined by two mountain men, Thomas ("Pegleg") Smith and Jim Beckwourth. In 1839–1840 his bands divided and he struck simultaneously at many ranches and carried off more than three thousand horses. The bitter Californio ranchers paid him the dubious tribute of being "the biggest horsethief in history." Walkara sold some horses to Jim Bridger; others were sent to Santa Fe.[21]

Walkara believed in diversification, so he raided Digger and Paiute villages for Indian women and chil-

20 See Francis Haines, *Horses in America* (New York: Thomas Y. Crowell, 1971); and Joseph J. Hill, "Spanish and Mexican Exploration and Trade Northwest from New Mexico into the Great Basin," *Utah Historical Quarterly* 3 (January, 1930), 3–23, 30–46.

21 The details of Walkara's life are treated in Paul Bailey, *Walkara, Hawk of the Mountains* (Los Angeles: Western Lore Press, 1954), and Conway B. Sonne, *The World of Walkara* (San Antonio: Naylor, 1962). See also Leland H. Creer, "Spanish-American Slave Trade in the Great Basin, 1800–1853," *New Mexico Historical Review* 24 (July, 1949), 171–183.

dren to be sold to New Mexicans. He liked the Mormons and traded with them. He also joined their church for, as other Indians had learned, "praying makes the pot boil." He was refused a white wife when he asked for one, however. When the Mormons stopped the slave trade and Americans came and ended the horse raids, Walkara fell on bad times. But he was impressive in power or out; it seemed appropriate that at his death fifteen horses were slaughtered on his grave.

If Walkara's obsession was horses, that of the Indian tribes of the Pacific Northwest coast was to acquire metal. From the mid-eighteenth century onward they sought iron, steel, and copper with an intensity that amazed observers. The coastal tribes already had a money system of sorts in dentalium shells secured in trade with California Indians. When Spanish vessels visiting the coast left a boat on shore or even a cross, each was smashed to bits for the ironwork it contained.[22] The Spanish chroniclers tell us that the natives objected to inferior iron and small knives. Since the coastal tribesmen practiced slavery, some chiefs employed their slaves to make special trade goods or collect furs that white traders would want. And just as the horse stimulated cultural and economic changes among the emerging Plains tribes, so knives stimulated an artistic and cultural boom in carved wooden objects in the Northwest.[23]

To the northwest, along the shores of Alaska, an-

[22] Warren L. Cook, *Flood Tide of Empire: Spain and the Pacific Northwest, 1543–1819* (New Haven: Yale University Press, 1973), pp. 75, 100–117. See also references to Chief Ma-kwee-na throughout.

[23] Both the culture of the Northwest tribes and their cultural takeoff are treated in Philip Drucker, *Indians of the Northwest Coast* (New York: McGraw-Hill, 1955).

other kind of exploitation developed in the eighteenth century when Russian merchants engaged in the sea otter fur trade brought the Aleut fishermen, who were adept at catching otter, into a form of indentured servitude. As the Russians pursued the dwindling herds southward, all the way to the islands off southern California, the dutiful Aleut fishermen went with them.[24]

From this bird's-eye view of the vast native-white trading frontiers of the trans-Mississippi West, several basic facts should be clear: first, that exploitative Indian-Indian and Indian-white trade in the West did not begin with American fur traders and Santa Fe merchants, but preceded actual white contact by generations. Second, we should see that the horse and the gun were not simply new tools of warfare and food gathering, but trade items themselves whose presence motivated warfare and intensified the trade impulse to the point that perhaps

24 Various aspects of the trade are treated in Hector Chevigny, *Russian America: The Great Alaskan Venture, 1749–1867* (New York: Viking Press, 1965); Semen B. Okun, *The Russian-American Company* (Cambridge, Mass.: Harvard University Press, 1951); and S. R. Tompkins, *Alaska, Promyshlennik and Sourdough* (Norman: University of Oklahoma Press, 1945).

more human beings were sold into slavery or exploited for reasons of trade than ever before. Although conditions were vastly different in the American South and the American West, there is perhaps a disturbing parallel in the way a desire for profits from tobacco and cotton promoted black slavery, and a desire for trade goods promoted various forms of bonded labor in the West.[25]

Ever since Frederick Jackson Turner wrote his famous essay, "The Significance of the Frontier in American History," in 1893, we have associated the frontier and wilderness with anarchic freedom, virginity, and democracy.[26] But if we look at the trans-Mississippi West in the decade 1830–1840, we discover a lively trade in Mexican and Indian captives in the Southwest, the practice of debt peonage in New Mexico, Indian peonage at the missions and on the ranches of California, the insti-

[25] For a distinguished treatment of the origins of the southern slave system, see Edmund S. Morgan, *American Slavery, American Freedom: The Ordeal of Colonial Virginia* (New York: W. W. Norton and Company, 1975). A broad discussion is David Brion Davis, *The Problem of Slavery in Western Culture* (Ithaca, N.Y.: Cornell University Press, 1966), and the same author's *The Problem of Slavery in the Age of Revolution, 1770–1823* (Ithaca, N.Y.: Cornell University Press, 1975).

[26] Frederick Jackson Turner, "The Significance of the Frontier in American History," in *The Frontier in American History* (New York: Henry Holt, 1920). Turner's association of frontier and democracy is explored in Howard R. Lamar, "Frederick Jackson Turner," in Marcus Cunliffe and Robin W. Winks, eds., *Pastmasters* (New York: Harper & Row, 1969).

tution of slavery in the Pacific Northwest, the indenture of Aleuts in Alaska, and the impressment of Hawaiian sailors (Kanakas) by American whaling and trading vessels.[27]

As we have noted earlier, one of the foremost practitioners of a raid-and-trade way of life in the mid-nineteenth century were the Comanches. With this fact in mind the theme of Charles W. Webber's novel, *Old Hicks, the Guide* (1848), which Henry Nash Smith so brilliantly analyzed in his book, *Virgin Land: The American West as Symbol and Myth* (1950), is indeed ironic. In *Old Hicks*, Webber depicted harmless Comanches living in Peaceful Valley on the Upper Canadian River. Then whites appeared who misled them into evil ways. But when left alone the Indians and nature were innocent.[28] Webber would probably have seen the white trader as one of the snakes in the Comanche Eden, but the fact is the trader's instinct was there before the whites came.

Long before Webber imagined his Comanche paradise, Thomas Jefferson dreamed that the American continent was truly a virgin land into which man could escape from evil by a proper use of the land to create a yeoman society. Lewis and Clark were to find that it was otherwise, a discovery which Robert Penn Warren has dramatized in his poem, *Brother to Dragons*, when he

27Arrell M. Gibson, *The West in the Life of the Nation* (Lexington, Mass.: Heath, 1976); L. R. Bailey, *Indian Slave Trade in the Southwest: A Study of Slave-taking and the Traffic in Indian Captives* (Los Angeles: Western Lore Press, 1966); Drucker, *Indians of the Northwest Coast*; and Robert F. Heizer and M. A. Whipple, eds., *The California Indians* (Berkeley: University of California Press, 1971).

28 Henry Nash Smith, *Virgin Land: The American West as Symbol and Myth* (Cambridge: Harvard University Press, 1950), pp. 72–77.

[27]

has Lewis return and say to Jefferson: "You sent me on a lie."[29]

It is not the intention of this essay to equate trade with wickedness, but to suggest that it has always existed in one form or another in the West. Thus, in our periodic re-examinations of the frontier, we should push our accounts of trade back in time and show maps of prehistoric Indian trade centers and routes, and then depict the Spanish, the French, the British, and the American ones. In the process we should take pains to balance those famous places like Fort Vancouver, Fort Laramie, Fort Union, and Bent's Fort with acknowledgments of the existence of Torrey's and Barnard's posts in Texas and other important ones that are not so well known. In such ways we can begin to discover a major medium through which red and white men first and most successfully communicated, for if the customer was not always right or was not always considered civilized, at least each side had to understand the other.[30]

Let us return to the Texas scene for a moment to see what took place after the Comanche and Kiowa were finally defeated in the 1870's and West Texas became a relatively safe place to live in. One of the first consequences was that Spanish Americans from New Mexico spread by the thousands onto the plains of Texas, Oklahoma, and Kansas to go into ranching and trading and

[29] Robert Penn Warren, *Brother to Dragons: A Tale in Verse and Voice* (New York: Random House, 1953). These same themes have been explored in John Logan Allen, *Passage Through the Garden* (Urbana: University of Illinois Press, 1975).

[30] This theme is explored more fully in Ewers, "The Influence of the Fur Trade," pp. 1–25, and in his "When Red and White Met," *Western Historical Quarterly* 2 (April, 1971), 133–150.

eventually into railroad work, which took them to Kansas City, Omaha, and other railroad centers.[31] It was an invisible "new frontier" that gets into cowboy songs but not into the history texts.

Not untypical was the little town of Tascosa in the Texas Panhandle, which consisted of a few stores around a plaza.[32] Before the Comanches' power was broken, they raided Texas herds on the Goodnight-Loving Trail. After their fall, ranches spread into the area, among them the famous LX ranch founded by Bates and Beals, who like the Torrey brothers were on-the-make New England Yankees. They, too, suffered from raids, not from Indians, but from cattle thieves, and especially from Billy the Kid's gang, which rode out from the Pecos Valley to steal cattle and horses to sell to unquestioning ranchers back in New Mexico.[33] At the same time from the eastern plains came the buffalo hunters armed with high-powered rifles. The latter not only wiped out the buffalo; in so doing they wiped out both the Indian's food supply and his basis of trade. While an ancient historic pattern of raid and trade with modern variations was continuing, the principals involved were no longer either Indian or Spanish.[34]

[31] D. W. Meinig, *Southwest: Three Peoples in Geographical Change, 1600–1970* (New York: Oxford University Press, 1971), pp. 27–37; John McCarty, *Maverick Town: The Story of Old Tascosa* (Norman: University of Oklahoma Press, 1946).

[32] Charles A. Siringo, *A Texas Cowboy* (Lincoln: University of Nebraska Press, 1950), p. 98, mentions Tascosa.

[33] Siringo, *A Texas Cowboy*, pp. 99–145 *passim*.

[34] J. Evetts Haley, "The Comanchero Trade," *Southwestern Historical Quarterly* 38 (January, 1935), 157–176, is a very perceptive account of these later "raid-and-trade" patterns. See also Kenner, *New Mexican–Plains Indian Relations*, chs. 8–9.

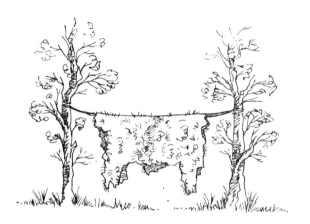

IN a recent article entitled "Stereotypes of the Mountain Man," Harvey L. Carter and Marcia C. Spencer drew the intriguing conclusion that their studies of the mountain men led them to believe that 60 percent of the fur traders in the Rocky Mountains were of French, French-Canadian, or French-Indian descent.[35] Such a statement provides the clue for the next distinctive period of the mythic trading frontier in the West. It was Pierre LaClede, a French trader from New Orleans, who, by chance or design, put it all together when he established St. Louis in 1764 as the most successful trading post in the history of the United States.[36] Symbolically, it was located almost on the site of one of the most elaborate and densely populated prehistoric Indian trading centers in the continental United States: Cahokia Mound.

[35] Harvey L. Carter and Marcia C. Spencer, "Stereotypes of the Mountain Man," *Western Historical Quarterly* 5 (January, 1975), 26 n.

[36] John Francis McDermott, *The Early Histories of St. Louis* (St. Louis: St. Louis Historical Documents Foundation, 1952).

Using St. Louis as a base, LaClede and his capable sons, the Chouteaus, began trading with the Indians west of the Mississippi. René Auguste and his brother Jean Pierre were in the Osage trade and later in the Missouri fur trade. In another generation Pierre Chouteau, Jr., was in the Upper Missouri trade and lead mining while his brother Auguste Pierre traded in frontier Oklahoma, where he lived like a frontier baron in a long palace with retainers and slaves. Some years before the first Americans appeared, Auguste Pierre traded so far into the Great Plains that the Spanish captured him and took him to Santa Fe.[37] By reaching up the Missouri to the Mandan trading center and southwestward to Santa Fe, the French and Spanish traders in St. Louis provide the missing link to the origins of the western American fur trade. They also provided something else: they were bicultural, and perhaps far more than David and John Torrey they understood and accepted their red customers. Auguste Pierre had Indian and white wives. If the customer was not always right, at least his sister was interesting.

The Chouteaus, however, were only one group among many French trading families and individuals operating on the Mississippi Valley frontier. The French had been trading across the Mississippi River on a two-thousand-mile front since the early eighteenth century. In 1713 Lamothe de Cadillac sent an intrepid Canadian lieutenant, Louis Juchereau de St. Denis, to found Natchitoches (Louisiana) and to trade into Texas and the

[37] John Francis McDermott, "Auguste Chouteau: First Citizen of Upper Louisiana," in McDermott, ed., *Frenchmen and French Ways in the Mississippi Valley* (Urbana: University of Illinois Press, 1969), pp. 1–14.

border provinces of Mexico. St. Denis soon got to the Rio Grande.[38] Two decades later Sieur de la Vérendrye had explored all the way from Canada to the Missouri, and by the 1790's Frenchmen were trying to trade up the Missouri from St. Louis.[39] Even when Americans came to dominate the fur trade after 1820, French traders and trappers continued to operate their own firms and were among the first to penetrate the Gila River region and the Great Basin.[40] And so, like persistent ghosts, the French names haunt the fur trade, begging recognition: Bernard and Sylvestre Pratte; Etienne Provost; Charles Larpenteur; Jean Baptiste Charbonneau, son of Sacajawea; Henri Chatillon, the dashing hunter-guide whom Parkman described so vividly in *The Oregon Trail*; the brothers Robidoux of Taos, and many others.[41]

Their bicultural approach—the classic stance of a frontier trader—was such that on the northern frontier the mixed bloods came to outnumber the pureblooded Indians before the trade era ended. Some went white, some went native, and some formed new communities that were neither white nor Indian and used log cabins and farmed. The change might express itself in the use

38 John Francis Bannon, *The Spanish Borderlands Frontier, 1513–1821* (New York: Holt, Rinehart and Winston, 1970), pp. 2, 110 ff.; Henri Folmer, "Contraband Trade between Louisiana and New Mexico in the Eighteenth Century," *New Mexico Historical Review* 16 (July, 1941), 249–274.

39 Abraham P. Nasatir, *Before Lewis and Clark* (St. Louis: St. Louis Historical Documents Foundation, 1952), 2 vols.

40 David J. Weber, *The Taos Trappers, 1540–1846* (Norman: University of Oklahoma Press, 1971).

41 Many of those with French surnames are described in Weber, *The Taos Trappers*. Others are treated in LeRoy R. Hafen, ed., *Mountain Men and the Fur Trade of the Far West* (Glendale, Calif.: Arthur H. Clark, 1965–1972), 10 vols.

of new floral as opposed to geometric designs in crafts, or there might be compromises: those farming might still go on an annual buffalo hunt.[42] In these instances trade meant acculturation but not necessarily defeat or deterioration of the tribes. Had the Americans not come, possibly a line of *metis* or halfbreeds would have existed from Oklahoma to Saskatchewan. Again the image of trader as destroyer is belied.

In his recent study of the Canadian frontier, W. J. Eccles has shifted the spotlight from heroes like Champlain and LaSalle to French merchants and trappers, whom he sees as paving the way for the expansion of the frontier. Eccles also finds that in Indian-white relations, Indian diplomacy was consistently better conceived and better executed than that of the European powers.[43] On the other side, it was the French technology of beaver trapping that started the rise of the most farflung enterprise in colonial North America. And it was the French *coureurs de bois* who first adjusted to the Indian and the wilderness and thus became, in effect, the first "mountain men," though they did not operate in mountainous country. In turn they taught the British in Canada how to live in the forest and to take Indian wives.[44]

By now the point should be obvious that the Indians, the French, and the British were all captivated by

42 Ewers, "The Influence of the Fur Trade"; Elwyn B. Robinson, *History of North Dakota* (Lincoln: University of Nebraska Press, 1966), pp. 20–98; Haines, *The Plains Indians*; Arthur J. Ray, *Indians in the Fur Trade: Their Role as Trappers, Hunters, and Middlemen in the Lands Southwest of Hudson Bay, 1660–1870* (Toronto; University of Toronto Press, 1974).

43 W. J. Eccles, *The Canadian Frontier, 1534–1760* (Albuquerque: University of New Mexico Press, 1974), pp. 103–131.

44 *Ibid.*; Harold A. Innis, *The Fur Trade in Canada* (New Haven: Yale University Press, 1930).

the life of the fur trade and its often surprising results. Rather than work to overturn it, they celebrated at the completion of the hunt and during the trading whether at a Montreal fair or a wilderness rendezvous. "Yet were I young again," said an old voyageur to Alexander Ross in 1825, "I should glory in commencing the same career again. I would spend another half-century in the same fields of enjoyment. There is no life as happy as a voyageur's life; none so independent; no place where a man enjoys so much variety and freedom as in the Indian country."[45]

As we come to the American period of trading and trapping on the Western frontier, we find that here the myths center on the nature of the Rocky Mountain fur trade and particularly on the mountain man. The Rocky Mountain system of fur trade has been praised for liberating the trade from the rivers and stationary posts by using horse-mounted brigades of trappers who stayed in the woods and did their trading once a year at wilderness rendezvous. In this system the trappers bypassed the Indian, which increased the red man's hostility and reduced his source of income for trade. The single-minded efficiency of the American fur trade system implied that it was not to be a permanent way of life but a temporary one, and it seems safe to say that even the wildest mountain man expected the plow to push aside the beaver.

The myth of the mountain man is a more complex story. In a series of historical exchanges that sometimes resemble the famous "when did you stop beating your

<hr />

[45] Alexander Ross, *The Fur Hunters of the West* (London, 1855), II, 236–237, as quoted in Eccles, *The Canadian Frontier*, p. 191.

wife" question, scholars and writers have argued as to whether the mountain man was, in the words of Harvey Carter, "a romantic hero, of legendary or epic proportions"; or a daring but degraded character who could not settle and thus fled to the farthest frontier "where he has sunk to the level of the savage inhabitants and lived a life free of moral restraint and financial responsibilities"; or whether he was, as William H. Goetzmann has described him, an expectant capitalist, hard-driving, ambitious, "eager to improve his status in society by the acquisition of wealth."[46]

One need not quarrel with categorizing mountain men and fur traders in this way, but the first two definitions assume the centrality of the wilderness and the fur-trapping experience, and imply—as did contemporary writers like Washington Irving, Lewis Garrard, and George Ruxton—that the fur trade created a special type of freak: a white savage who gloried in anarchic freedom or who liked killing and scalping. It was assumed that, like a specialized dinosaur, they would die when their special environment collapsed. Such reasoning makes it

46 Carter and Spencer, "Stereotypes of the Mountain Man," pp. 17–18. The description of the "expectant capitalist" quoted above are Carter and Spencer's words, not Goetzmann's. See William H. Goetzmann, "The Mountain Man as Jacksonian Man," *American Quarterly* 15 (Fall, 1963), 402–415.

apparent that they have been the major victims of romantic myths about the innocence and wildness of nature, cults about romantic primitivism, the American belief in progress, and a prudish Victorian fear of miscegenation.[47] The very biculturalism that the French traders practiced became in the mountain men either repulsive depravity or extreme romance.[48] The treatment of mountain men by American writers, diarists, and observers in the nineteenth century is as much an index to our cultural norms as Roy Harvey Pearce's account of white response to Indians in his *Savages and Savagism*. Indeed, the taboo against an Indian life style was remarkably similar to the taboos against the way mountain men lived.

It behooves us to find ways by which we can provide the mountain man with a means of escape from his Rocky Mountain wilderness cage. We might ask first about the origins of certain well-known but representative mountain men.[49] Major Andrew Henry and Zenas Leonard were from Pennsylvania. William Ashley, Jim Bridger, and Joe Meek were Virginians. Thomas Fitzpatrick and Robert Campbell were from Ireland. We find equally diverse origins among the French trappers: Charles Larpenteur was from Fountainbleau in his native France. Antoine Robidoux was French Canadian.

[47] One need only read the novels of James Fenimore Cooper to find these themes.

[48] Overland diarists were usually intrigued or horrified when they met a halfbreed or a man with an Indian or a Mexican wife.

[49] Information about the various mountain men cited in the list was obtained from Hafen, *Mountain Men*, and from entries contributed by Gordon S. Dodds to Howard R. Lamar, ed., *Reader's Encyclopedia of the American West* (New York: Thomas L. Crowell, forthcoming, 1977).

Ceran St. Vrain, partner of the Bents, was born of French nobility in Missouri. What made the fur frontier so fascinating was not that they were all alike, but that they came from such diverse sources. It was a leather-clad foreign legion of all types and classes.

Lewis Garrard in *Wah-To-Yah and the Taos Trail* has given us the impression that all social bonds were dissolved in the mountain man's world, that he was the supreme individualist.[50] Yet we find that the five Sublette brothers, the four Bent brothers, Joseph Walker and his brothers, the innumerable Chouteaus, the Robidoux brothers (some six in number), and Joseph Meek and his two brothers were all in the trade, or related trades, together. Not too surprisingly, blood ties counted, but so did marriage ties. Recent prosographical studies of mountain men indicate that 84 percent were married, of which number 36 percent were married to Indians and 34 percent to whites of Mexican extraction, a category nineteenth-century Americans considered nonwhite.[51] What can we deduce from these bare statistics? Since most mountain men left no record and we have but the sketchiest accounts of the wives of those with records, arguments about whether they were degraded or noble seem useless. It does seem reasonable to argue, however, that if we know how frontier trade systems have always worked from time immemorial, and if we know how extended families worked and behaved in preindustrial societies, and if we see how the traditional

50 Lewis H. Garrard, *Wah-To-Yah and the Taos Trail* (1850), reprinted in 1938 as volume six in the Southwest Historical Series (Glendale, Calif.: Arthur H. Clark), with an introduction by Ralph P. Bieber.

51 Richard J. Fehrman, "The Mountain—A Statistical View," in Hafen, *Mountain Men*, X, 11–12.

French bi-cultural approach worked in North America —as well as how a half-breed society functions—we might begin to understand not only the mountain man, but also the trader and the American fur trade itself.

As a further test of the mythic accounts we must also study the nature of hunting and trapping. To comprehend the philosophy of a scavenging existence and the nature of the chase is to comprehend certain forms of frontier violence which arise when human beings come to view other human beings as quarry. Richard Slotkin, in his *Regeneration Through Violence*, has begun to explain this hunting attitude and the sense of power through killing—or through reducing the wilderness—in such a way that it does indeed seem as American as apple pie.[52]

Next, it seems in order to differentiate mountain men not only by background and attitude, but also by age difference and generational attitudes. Major Andrew Henry was born in 1775, and his partner in the Rocky Mountain fur trade, William H. Ashley, was born in 1778. They came from a generation which knew the older systems of the fur trade, and in Missouri they came to know French ways. Ashley, once he was successful, lived grandly like the Chouteaus or a rich fur merchant of Montreal. What might be called a "second generation," born around 1798–1800, included Jedediah Smith, Charles Bent, Joseph Reddeford Walker, James Clyman, and William Sublette. That remarkable group was followed by an equally impressive "third genera-

---

[52] Richard Slotkin, *Regeneration Through Violence: The Mythology of the American Frontier, 1600–1860* (Middletown, Conn.: Wesleyan University Press, 1973).

tion consisting of Jim Bridger, Zenas Leonard, William Bent, Kit Carson, Joe Meek, and Robert Campbell. Still another generation, in which "Uncle Dick" Wootton, Jim Baker, and William T. Hamilton could be found, was born between 1816 and 1822. Reporters interviewing the last three near the end of the nineteenth century have given us some of our most exaggerated accounts of the mountain man.

Finally, one might look at their total careers. The assumption has always existed that the mountain men were locked into a single exciting job, and that when it ended they were left broken and disoriented. The fact is that the hunting-gathering existence can take many forms. It is, so the anthropologists tell us, an efficient and flexible form of survival.[53] At the same time the trader, whether on the frontier or in the city, is also flexible. Jedediah Smith, the greatest of the mountain men, had already switched to the Santa Fe trade when he was killed by Charles Webber's innocent Comanches at a waterhole near the Cimarron.[54] Henry and Ashley were in other businesses besides fur trading. In these men and others we can see a powerful combination of the scavenger-hunter and the mercantile mind which turned them into talented jacks-of-all-trades.

Yet we can never destroy the myth. Despite the fact

[53] The "efficiency" of the hunting and gathering economy has been treated in Robert F. Spencer, Jesse Jennings, *et al.*, *The Native Americans: Prehistory and Ethnology of the North American Indians* (New York: Harper and Row, 1965), and more recently in J. R. Harlan, "The Plants and Animals That Nourish Man," *Scientific American* 235 (September, 1976), 89–97.

[54] Dale Morgan, *Jedediah Smith and the Opening of the West* (Indianapolis, Ohio: Bobbs-Merrill, 1953).

that many mountain men, including Jedediah Smith, were clean-shaven and wore regular American clothes, the image of Francis Parkman's Henri Chatillon, with his drooping felt hat, fringed deerskin leggings and moccasins, armed with a rifle and a knife, will not go away.[55] Thus we must recognize and analyze what it was in our society after 1822 and down to the present that makes us make them a frontier myth. Part of it can be explained by the Victorian romanticism of the nineteenth century. But a major part stems from the fact that we can still go into the woods today and experience the thrill of hunting, danger, and death. It is simply a variation of the eternal adventure story, American-style.

Meanwhile we are encountering a new mythic mountain man in the popular genre of wilderness movies. As millions see *Jeremiah Johnson, A Man Called Horse,* or the adventures of a family in the wilderness, once again the issue arises: is that life degraded or noble, monstrous or kindly primitive? The point the historian must make is that they were not necessarily either, but rather a variety of human beings living in a fascinating world which combined the scavenger-hunting lifestyle with mercantile capitalism.

[55] For a brief biography of Chatillon, see Wilbur R. Jacobs, "Henri Chatillon," in Hafen, *Mountain Men,* I, 229–231, but the image was set, of course, in Francis Parkman's *The Oregon Trail* (1849).

As an epilogue to the story of the mountain man–fur trader, let us consider the cowboy, who is another one of myth's victims. His mythic and symbolic image is, in fact, even more powerful than that of the mountain man. There are qualities in the cowboy life that were present in the mountain man that throw still more light on the role of the trader on the American frontier. It seems appropriate to look at one of the molders of the cowboy image, Charles A. Siringo, a pintsized but fearless Texan born on Matagorda Bay in 1855. Thirty years later Siringo wrote *A Texas Cowboy, or Fifteen Years on the Hurricane Deck of a Spanish Pony*.[56] It was the first cowboy autobiography to be published, and it contained all the elements of the open-range cattle industry and the cowboy saga that have become standard fare for fiction and film.

Somewhat like Kit Carson or Jim Bridger, Siringo had a talent for meeting interesting people in interesting places. At sixteen he went to work for Abel Head ("Shanghai") Pierce, the Rhode Island–born rancher in southern Texas who boasted that his spread was so large the Gulf of Mexico was his drift fence. Siringo's childhood and life in the Matagorda Bay area was first a scavenger existence. His father died when he was one and left his family destitute. Young Charlie hunted game for food and whenever the opportunity arose, he and

[56] A convenient sketch of Siringo is Charles D. Peavy, *Charles A. Siringo, A Texas Picaro* (Austin: Steck-Vaughn Company, 1967), but also useful is a brief account of Siringo and a bibliography of his works by J. Frank Dobie in Charles A. Siringo, *A Texas Cowboy* (Lincoln: University of Nebraska Press, 1950).

his mother salvaged items from ships wrecked on Matagorda Peninsula. Local cowboys killed and skinned maverick cattle for their hides. Nearby at Indianola three factories were busy packing turtles for shipment and sale.[57]

Scavenging could take many forms. The first time Siringo met Shanghai Pierce, the latter had just purchased stolen Mexican ponies for two dollars a head with no questions asked. Siringo soon learned that everyone was engaged in doing a little branding on the side to build up a herd separate from that of the boss. After heavy coastal floods Siringo and his friends skinned drowned cattle and sold the hides to local firms. He learned to horsetrade as well, for Siringo wanted money and a ranch of his own. He was a frontier expectant capitalist, but he also wanted fun and excitement, so he swapped outfits, worked on the various cattle trails, and once, while in Dodge City, had the honor of being hit on the head by a beer mug wielded by Bat Masterson, who also worked as a bartender when not on duty as a deputy.[58]

Siringo then herded cattle in the Texas Panhandle for the LX ranch. There he befriended Billy the Kid, who, so says Siringo, asked him to join his gang. The outfit he worked for itself sometimes put its brand on the wrong cows. One of the foremen, Bill Moore, was a

[57] Siringo, *A Texas Cowboy*, pp. 7–17, 41–50; Junann J. Stieghorst, *Bay City and Matagorda County* (Austin: Pemberton Press, 1965).

[58] The Bat Masterson episode is mentioned in Siringo's *A Cowboy Detective* (Chicago: W. B. Conkey Company, 1912), and in his *Riata and Spurs* (Cambridge, Mass.: Houghton Mifflin, 1927), but is also detailed in Chester Newton Hess, "Sagebrush Sleuth: The Saga of Charlie Siringo," *New Mexico Sun Trails* 7 (1952), 2–4, 11–13.

murderer. But Siringo also had the pleasure of knowing Henry F. Hoyt, a young physician who gave up his practice for a time to experience the romance and adventure of being a cowboy. Another one of Siringo's bunkmates was Jim East, who later became famous as the sheriff of Tascosa.[59] Add to this an assortment of Mexican and Anglo-American trail hands and one has a gathering of adventurous youths not unlike those who came to the Green River fur trade rendezvous during the 1830's.

Siringo refused Billy the Kid's offer and went, instead, to the Kansas cattle town of Caldwell, where he ran a cigar store, an ice cream parlor, and an oyster bar while writing up his cowboy career. He explained that the resulting volume, *A Texas Cowboy*, was written to make money "and lots of it." Although it was hawked as a thirty-cent wonder by news butchers on trains for many years and eventually sold a million copies, it did not make Siringo rich. But his book, Owen Wister's *The Virginian*, and Andy Adams' *Log of a Cowboy* have played a major role in shaping the cowboy image for all time.[60]

Siringo then went on to have a second career as exciting as his first. From 1886 to 1908 he worked as a Pinkerton detective out of the agency's regional office in Denver.[61] Using techniques of tracking stolen cattle

59 J. Evetts Haley, "Jim East—Trail Hand and Cowboy," *Panhandle-Plains Historical Review* 4 (Canyon, Texas, 1931); and Henry F. Hoyt, *A Frontier Doctor* (Boston and New York: Houghton Mifflin, 1929).

60 Andy Adams, *Log of a Cowboy* (Boston and New York: Houghton-Mifflin, 1903); Owen Wister, *The Virginian* (New York: Macmillan, 1902).

61 The episodes in this and succeeding paragraphs are detailed in Siringo's *A Cowboy Detective*.

learned in Texas and adopting aliases with total ease, he successfully tracked down rustlers and bank robbers, joined gangs to get the goods on their ringleaders, and even chased Butch Cassidy and the Sun Dance Kid. In 1892 he penetrated a local miners' union in the Coeur d'Alene region of Idaho by posing as a pro-union laborer. His disguise was so successful he became secretary to the union and was able to send all the union's plans to his employer, the miner owners, by mail. When the union leaders discovered Siringo was a double agent, they were so furious they blew up the company mine at Gem, Idaho, and tried to find and kill the hapless detective. Siringo escaped by crawling a quarter of a mile under a board sidewalk to safety—one thinks of Hugh Glass's famous crawl through the wilderness—as the cursing miners were hunting for him immediately overhead.[62]

[62] Siringo's activities as double agent in the Coeur d'Alene region have been sympathetically portrayed in William T. Stoll, *Silver Strike* (Boston: Little, Brown, 1932). Glass's ordeal has been treated in John G. Neihardt, *The Song of Hugh Glass* (New York: Macmillan, 1915), and in Frederick Manfred, *Lord Grizzly* (New York: Signet, New American Library, 1954).

Charles Siringo's career was that of a hunting and gathering trickster-trader. His West was one where men, whether rich or poor, scrounged for a living by hunting down and branding wild cattle as their own or by stripping skins for sale. On one occasion Siringo's boss sold unsuspecting buyers wild cattle that he knew would stampede and return home to be sold again. For the whole of his life Siringo lived on an actual and psychological borderland where morality counted for little and where hunting for men as well as animals was bound to provoke violence. Still, at the same time, it provided excitement, heroes and villains, and even romance.[63] Siringo's conditioning and his career give us a latter-day insight into frontier attitudes held by many of the fur traders and trappers, and his career also tells us much about the problem of law and order and violence on the frontier.

Even after Siringo went to work for the Pinkerton Detective Agency (we might read John Jacob Astor's American Fur Company here), he overcharged the customer, padded his expense account, and for a long time did not question whether he was pursuing his quarry for reasons of law and order, for justice, or simply because he was a hired gun. His career helps explain why there was so much violence in the West because the so-called law and order forces were sometimes as violent or as corrupt as the criminals who broke the law.[64]

63 Slotkin, *Regeneration Through Violence.*

64 The excesses of violence are detailed in W. Eugene Hollon, *Frontier Violence: Another Look* (New York: Oxford University Press, 1974); Wayne Gard, *Frontier Justice* (Norman: University of Oklahoma Press, 1949); and Richard Maxwell Brown, *Strain of Violence: Historical Studies of American Violence and Vigilantism* (New York: Oxford University Press, 1975).

Many observers have concluded that Siringo did not have much of a conscience.[65] Still, he was absolutely fearless, and though he was a dead shot with his Colt forty-five, he seldom used it. He was also a delightful fellow, a boon companion, and a sweet talker to the ladies. He was married four times. In 1907 something happened to Siringo while he was listening to Clarence Darrow defend the officials of the Western Federation of Miners whom Siringo and his superior, detective James McParland, had helped put in jail. At the famous trial of Big Bill Haywood at Boise in 1905–1907, Siringo, aged fifty-two, had a twinge of conscience as Darrow told the jury how the little man and the worker had been put upon by mine owners and detectives. In 1908 he began to dissociate himself from the Pinkertons. He wrote up his experiences and tried to publish them in 1912 under the title, *A Cowboy Detective*. Again his stated purpose was to make money. But the agency, nervous about what one of their most talented agents might reveal, seized the book plates by court order. The volume was not published until Siringo disguised the names of real persons mentioned in the volume. From then on Siringo lived the life of a hunted man, constantly under threat of extradition for libel.[66] Siringo's attitudes, his incredible adventures, and his mobility echo those of the mountain man. His wilderness included cities and

65 Siringo's "philosophy" is discussed in Neil M. Clark, "Close Calls: An Interview with Charles A. Siringo," *The American Magazine*, January, 1929.
66 Siringo eventually denounced his former employer in his *Two Evil Isms: Pinkertonism and Anarchism* (Chicago: Charles A. Siringo, 1915), a pamphlet which, like his book *A Cowboy Detective*, involved him in libel suits.

courts, but it was dangerous and full of adventure.

Like Wyatt Earp, John P. Clum, and Emmett Dalton, Siringo was so self-conscious about his colorful past and the fact that it might be sold that he drifted to Hollywood in the 1920's. Though old and ailing, he got a job as an extra in one of William S. Hart's westerns.[67] The cycle was complete. The creator of the cowboy image was now engulfed by the romantic myth as he, bent by arthritis and suffering from a hacking cough, acted out his bit part in Hart's famous *Tumbleweeds*.[68]

[67] The details of Siringo's last days are gleaned from a series of letters written between 1923 and 1927 to Alois M. Renehan, his lawyer in Santa Fe. See Alois M. Renehan Papers, Mss. in Archives in New Mexico, Santa Fe. See also interview with Siringo in Los Angeles *Evening Express*, April 11, 1927.

[68] *Tumbleweeds* was the story of the coming of the "sooners" and "boomers" to Oklahoma.

Just as Kit Carson became confined within his own myth
by reading books about himself, Siringo was now confined to the Hollywood western. Failing to make money
off his last book, *Riata and Spurs*, he lived out his last
days in a cabin in Los Angeles. There death came to him
as he was building a camper so he could retrace and
mark the Old Chisholm Trail.[69] He spoke of those days
on the trail as the old voyageur had spoken to Alexander
Ross about his days in the fur trade.

[69] Siringo's desire to mark the Chisholm Trail was longstanding.
He had mentioned the project to William E. Hawks just before World
War I and continued to mention it throughout the 1920's in his cor-
respondence with Hawks. See William E. Hawks Letters, Mss. in Bei-
necke Library, Yale University. Hawks, a collector of folklore and cowboy songs, bought songs that Siringo had copied down on the trail.

As the frontier receded and the trading post and the cattle town disappeared, a new kind of trader appeared: the wholesale commission merchant who supplied army posts or smaller local stores by freight wagon or by train. The bicultural firm of Otero and Seller operated in territorial New Mexico, as did the firm of Charles Ilfeld, a Jewish immigrant in New Mexico. In Arizona two firms, Lord and Williams and Tully and Ochoa dominated the territory's mercantile economy for a time.[70] In San Francisco the powerful Parrott Company supplied firms in Nevada and Arizona.[71] In Wyoming everyone was aware that Senator Francis E. Warren's wholesale company was but the tip of a pyramid of business enterprises. In Montana the Missoula Mercantile Company, founded in the nineteenth century, still exists, as does ZCMI, the century-old department store in Salt Lake City.[72]

When the western trader evolved from scavenger-exploiter to merchant-developer, his customers changed from Indians and frontiersmen to white settlers. It may

70 I have explored the theme of mercantile capitalism in greater detail in Howard R. Lamar, "Persistent Frontier: The West in the Twentieth Century," *Western Historical Quarterly* 4 (January, 1973), 11–16; and Lamar, *The Far Southwest, 1846–1912* (New Haven: Yale University Press, 1966), pp. 107, 142, 172, 198, 452–454. See also William J. Parish, *The Charles Ilfeld Company: A Study of the Rise and Decline of Merchant Capitalism in New Mexico* (Cambridge, Mass.: Harvard University Press, 1961).

71 William H. Hutchinson, "California's Economic Imperialism: An Historical Iceberg," in John A. Carroll, ed., *Reflections of Western Historians* (Tucson: University of Arizona Press, 1969).

72 Lewis L. Gould, *Wyoming: A Political History, 1868–1896* (New Haven: Yale University Press, 1968), p. 79; Leonard J. Arrington, *Great Basin Kingdom* (Cambridge, Mass.: Harvard University Press, 1958).

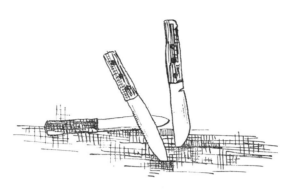

be more than a half-truth to say that Neiman-Marcus is now serving demanding Texans just as the Torrey Brothers once served the Comanches. However great the change, there was continuity. In 1859, old Louis Vasquez, Jim Bridger's veteran partner at Bridger's Fort, sent his nephew to gold-rush Denver with goods to supply the Pikes Peakers.[73] Jim Beckwourth, black mountain man and once a chief of the Crows, set up a hotel in the Sierras on one of the main roads to the California mines.[74] Jim Baker, one of the wildest looking of mountain men, operated a store at the Green River Crossing of the Mormon Trail, but when gold was discovered in the Pike's Peak region, he set up a store in Denver, built a toll bridge, and ran a ranch before becoming a guide and interpreter for the Ute Indian Agency.[75] Mountain

[73] Dale L. Morgan and Eleanor T. Harris, eds., *Rocky Mountain Journal of William Marshall Anderson* (San Marino: Henry E. Huntington Library, 1967); and Gordon S. Dodds, "Louis Vasquez" in Lamar, ed., *Reader's Encyclopedia of the American West.*

[74] Charles G. Leland, ed., *The Life and Adventures of James P. Beckwourth* (1892); and Elinor Wilson, *Jim Beckwourth, Black Mountain Man and War Chief of the Crows* (Norman: University of Oklahoma Press, 1972).

[75] Nolie Mumey, *The Life of Jim Baker, 1818–1898: Trapper, Scout, Guide and Indian Fighter* (Denver: The World Press, 1931).

man "Uncle Dick" Wootton ran a trading post in Denver as well as a saloon and hotel before building his famous toll road over Raton Pass.[76]

The story of the merchant-trader runs right to the present in some parts of the West. In 1886 David and William Babbitt, two brothers in the grocery and hardware business in Cincinnati, bought a ranch in Flagstaff, Arizona, on the Atlantic and Pacific Railroad. David and another brother, George, ran a store there while William and brother Charles managed the ranch. By 1889 the Babbitt Brothers Trading Company had expanded into sheep raising, real estate, ice and meat-packing, and had bought the remnant herd of the Aztec Land and Cattle Company.[77] In many ways they were doing what Charles and William Bent were doing at Bent's Fort and Dr. John McLoughlin was doing at Fort Vancouver, Oregon, a half century before. Eventually the Babbitts established branch stores at Holbrook, Winslow, Williams, and Kingman. They also opened Indian trading posts at Red Lake, Willow Springs, and Tuba City. By 1918 the company had automobile dealerships in Phoenix, Tucson, and El Paso. Three of the brothers went into politics as had mountain men Ashley, Sublette, and Joe Meek. By 1960 the Babbitt enterprises included a chain of supermarkets, seven Indian posts, four cattle ranches, and still other operations. A similar story of evolution could be told about two other frontier merchant firms in Arizona: the Goldwater stores and the

[76] H. L. Conard, *Uncle Dick Wootton* (Chicago, 1890); Harvey L. Carter, "Richens Lacy Wootton," in Hafen, *The Mountain Men*, III.

[77] Harwood Hinton, "The Babbit Family," in *Reader's Encyclopedia of the American West*; and Edward H. Peplow, *History of Arizona*, 3 vols. (New York: Lewis Historical Pub. Co., 1958), III, 428–429.

business enterprises of the late Senator Carl Hayden.[78]

In re-examining the frontier we need to know more about the elusive and flexible frontier trader, his attitudes and his world, for in many instances he was more of a key figure in Indian history than the missionary was.[79] There was, as Meriwether Lewis knew, a fundamental contradiction in Jefferson's dream. The sage of Monticello hoped that the trader would be replaced by the self-sufficient farmer and that the Indian himself would be assimilated and become a farmer. Unlike most of his countrymen, Jefferson even thought that reds and whites should marry so that they would become one people.[80] What he did not understand was that the Indian was Indian and that trade was the one successful means of communication between the world of the Indian and the world of the white. The trader, however hostile, had to know and tolerate two worlds, whereas the farmer did not, for he had no need for the Indian. What Jefferson seemed to deny was that trade itself was exciting, romantic, dangerous—and profitable. Combined with the thrill of the chase it was an inevitable and attractive part of the human condition. The combination was, in fact, a major ingredient of a unique and vigorous emerging

[78] Bert M. Fireman, "Charles Trumbull Hayden," *Smoke Signal* 19 (Tucson Westerners, Spring, 1969); Richard Carlson, "Goldwaters; Merchants since 1862," *Arizona Highways* 15 (May 1939), 6–7, 26–27.

[79] In addition to articles by Ewers and Haley cited above and such classics as Josiah Gregg, *Commerce of the Prairies*, 2 vol. (1844; annotated edition by Max L. Moorhead, 1954), see McNitt, *The Indian Traders*; Kenner, *New Mexican–Plains Indian Relations*; and Lewis O. Saum, *The Fur Trader and the Indian* (Seattle: University of Washington Press, 1965).

[80] Jefferson's views on assimilation are discussed in Reginald Horsman, *Expansion and American Indian Policy, 1783–1812* (East Lansing: Michigan State University Press, 1967).

American culture. Lewis and Clark were sent to open a passage to India and to spy out new homesteads for American farmers.[81] What they did was to open up new franchise areas for the Indian trade. Frontier and West were, and are, two symbols of the special Indian and trader's world that resulted. And however devastating the outcome, everyone agreed that the beaver was more fun than the plow.

81 Allen, *Passage Through the Garden.*